Awfully Ancient

Thomas Crapper, Corsets, and Cruel Britannia

A Grim History of the Vexing Victorians!

Peter Hepplewhite

Gareth Stevens
PUBLISHING

Please visit our website, **www.garethstevens.com**.
For a free color catalog of all our high-quality books,
call toll-free 1-800-542-2595 or fax 1-877-542-2596.

Library of Congress Cataloging-in-Publication Data
Hepplewhite, Peter.
Thomas Crapper, corsets, and the cruel Britannia: a grim
history of the vexing Victorians! / by Peter Hepplewhite.
p. cm. — (Awfully ancient)
Includes index.
ISBN 978-1-4824-3133-9 (pbk.)
ISBN 978-1-4824-3136-0 (6 pack)
ISBN 978-1-4824-3134-6 (library binding)
1. Great Britain — History — Victoria, 1837-1901 — Juvenile
literature. 2. Great Britain — Social life and customs —
19th century — Juvenile literature. I. Hepplewhite, Peter.
II. Title.
DA550.H47 2016
941.081—d23

Published in 2016 by
Gareth Stevens Publishing
111 East 14th Street, Suite 349
New York, NY 10003

Copyright © Wayland / Gareth Stevens 2016

Senior editor: Julia Adams
Illustrator: Tom Morgan-Jones
Designer: Rocket Design (East Anglia) Ltd.

Manufactured in the United States of America
CPSIA compliance information: Batch #CS15GS.
For further information contact Gareth Stevens, New York, New York at 1-800-542-2595.

Ever suffered from
smelly curtains?
Turn to page 14 to
find out more...

The Victorian era was
the age of steam, but
it was also the age of
coal, mega-loads of
it, and there's no fire
without smoke (or
something like that).
Turn to page 12 for
the smoky facts!

Fancy a pie? – Yes please!
How about one made with
sparrows?

Contents

Fried mouse medicine – page 6

Jubilee Joy

In 1897, the Victorians went wild for Queen Victoria's Diamond Jubilee celebrations. Queen Vic had reigned for 60 incredible years — and people were already calling the 19th century the Victorian era!

Britain was nicknamed the *workshop of the world,* with trade worth £1.5 billion ($2.27 billion) in 1901, and a global empire of 410 million people. BUT this came at a cost...

American author Mark Twain visited London for the Jubilee celebrations and wrote:

The world has moved farther ahead since the Queen was born than it moved in the last 2000 years put together.

Cor blimey, gov!

It's the rich what get the gravy
And the poor what get the blame
It's the same the whole world over,
Ain't that a blooming shame!

Victorian Music Hall Song, about 1890

He was right. The Victorians were the first to face many of the problems of the modern world, and sometimes this made life really, really, really tough for ordinary folks.

Troubling times

Victorian Britain was deeply unfair: most of the nation's wealth was owned by just 5 percent of the people, while 40 percent were bitterly poor.

The population in Britain exploded from 10.5 million in 1801 to 38 million in 1901. London became the first megacity with 7 million people by 1901.

In 1851, for the first time anywhere in the world, more people lived in towns than in the countryside. But the booming cities were full of smoke-choked slums, with no sewers and piles of poop everywhere! One in five babies died before they were a year old and killer diseases ran riot. Doctors didn't help — almost half the patients who had an operation died from infections.

Victorian cities were choking with stinky smoke from factories and houses.

VERY VEXING VICTORIANS

Workhouse scandal

Many poor people were sent to workhouses. In Andover, they were so badly fed they started eating bones that had been brought in to make fertilizer.

Mr. Wakely: *What work were you employed at in the workhouse?*

Charles Lewis: *I was employed in breaking bones.*

Mr. Wakely: *Did you ever see men gnaw anything from these bones?*

Charles Lewis: *I have seen them eat the marrow out of these bones.*

Report to Parliament, 1846

Chilling Childhood

Cor blimey, gov!

A folk cure for whooping cough: feed your baby fried mouse. No, this isn't ancient Egypt – this is Britain 150 years ago!

Being born a Victorian was a killer. One out of every 10 new moms died giving birth or from infections within a few weeks of having a baby. And where did the infections come from? The dirty hands of the doctor or midwife who helped deliver the baby.

The first doctor who worked this out was Ignaz Semmelweis in Vienna. In 1847, he ordered his students to wash their hands in calcium chloride before examining new mothers and their babies. The death rate fell from 30 moms in 100 to three in 100! And what was his reward? Ignaz was fired for having "stupid ideas"!

Baby, be careful

Babies didn't have a great time either. One in every five died before they were a year old from an onslaught of evils. Many caught childhood diseases such as measles or scarlet fever, while others died from eating poor quality food or drinking infected water. Tummy bugs that caused diarrhea, and lung infections such as bronchitis, were the biggest causes of death.

Intoxicated infants

Most Victorians knew little about bringing up babies and ill-treated them through ignorance.

VERY VEXING VICTORIANS

Baby beware: your milk will make you sick!

Victorian baby bottles had cute names like *My Little Pet*, but the designs were a disaster. Rubber tubes and teats were attached to curved glass bottles. None of these parts could be cleaned properly, so the health-endangering bacteria blossomed.

Busy mothers doped infants with opium-based drugs to make them sleepy. These tinctures were sold over the counter and had comforting names such as *Street's Infant Quietness*; but if the dose was wrong, little Albert or Alice never woke up.

Other babies were drugged so often they couldn't eat properly and wasted away from malnutrition. And how about this rotten recipe for weaning babies: soggy bread, water, sugar, molasses, and milk? Very nourishing!

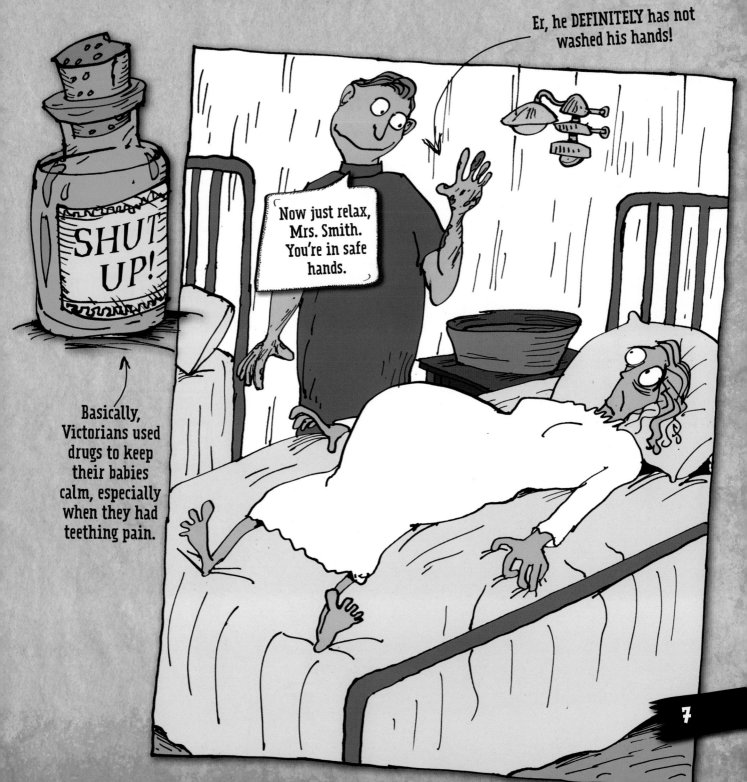

Basically, Victorians used drugs to keep their babies calm, especially when they had teething pain.

Cruel Schools

Victorian teachers went into the classroom with two popular sayings in mind: "Children should be seen and not heard" and "Spare the rod and spoil the child." Yep, the kids sure didn't have an easy life in school.

No view for you

Victorian schools could be quite dingy and joyless. Windows were high up, so the children wouldn't be distracted by the goings–on outside. Pupils sat in rows of varnished wooden desks

Typical Victorian classroom PRISON!

Cane

Grumpy old teacher

High window so you can't see out

Terrified kids

THWAK! A smack on the bum with a tawse (leather strap) would bring a tear to the eye.

VERY VEXING VICTORIANS

These kids found fame in the punishment book for St. Peters School in Alvescot, Oxfordshire, during summer term 1901.

First name	Surname	Reason for punishment	Punishment
Walter	Peachey	Causing disorder in line; being dismissed	two straps
Harry	Walker	Repeated disobedience to teacher	three straps
George	Simpson	Disorder for the second time in the assembly line	one strap
Cecil	Flux	Chipping school desk	two straps
Frank	Walker	Disorder when teacher was away from class	two straps
Beatrice	Taylor	Disorder when teacher was away from class	one strap

facing the blackboard. Sometimes large halls held several noisy classes side-by-side.

The most important lessons were the "three Rs" – Reading, wRiting and aRithmetic. Lessons were humdrum, with lots of repetition. Children chanted lists of kings and queens, capital cities of the world, and tables of weights and measures.

Wet cane – what a pain

To keep control, teachers used a cane to punish pupils, usually on the hands or the bum. Scottish teachers preferred a leather strap called the tawse. Believe it or not, some terribly terrifying teachers kept birch wood canes in buckets of water, so the wood stayed supple and hurt more.

However, teachers faced punishment, too — from parents. *The Schoolmistress,* a newspaper for teachers, complained: *the rough language and violence heaped on teachers in rough neighborhoods can hardly be imagined.* Only fair, do we hear you say?

Rocking reform

The 1870 Education Act made school places available for every child in the country between the ages of 5 and 10. In 1872, there were 38,000 teachers; by 1888 this had swelled to an army of 100,000.

THWAK! The birch cane was already a pain, but soaking it in water was really nasty!

Wearying Work

Cotton reels

The Industrial Revolution was powered by steam engines — and children. No, they weren't burned instead of coal; kids were employed in most key industries, including cotton mills, coal mines, and iron works.

Climbing boys

Perhaps the unluckiest children were the climbing boys. They were employed by sweeps to scramble up chimneys and brush them clean. The smaller and skinnier the child, the better. They were often burned in hot flues, and sometimes suffocated by falls of soot. Boys who got stuck were dragged back down with ropes tied to their ankles.

In big coal mines, children made up a third of the workforce. Bizarrely, the youngest kids — and some were only five or six — operated safety equipment. These tiny trappers opened and closed wooden trapdoors to circulate fresh air and stop the buildup of explosive or poisonous gases. They worked the same shifts as the men who cut the coal, 12 hours a day, six days a week.

Trappers

Only another 7 hours to go, Jack!

Can't we have a tea break?

Mill girls

Girls only had it a little better. Many worked as domestic servants. But don't think that they were housemaids in stately homes. Most girls were skivvies (menial housemaids) for families who could only afford one servant. They did the washing, cleaning, shopping, and often cooking, too.

In the north of England, young mill girls started as piecers. They scrambled under working looms to clean up cotton waste and repair broken threads. If a girl's hair was caught, it was ripped from her

VERY VEXING VICTORIANS

Fanny Drake, aged 15, pit lass

I work at Charlesworth's Wood Pit in Wakefield. I hurry (push coal tubs) by myself. I don't like it so well. It's cold and there is no fire in the pit. I'd rather be out of it altogether. I push with my head sometimes; it makes my head so sore that I cannot bear it to be touched.

scalp — if she was lucky. If not, she was dragged into the loom and crushed. The 1842 Mines Act banned children under 11 and all girls and women from working underground.

11

Killer Coal

The age of steam was also the age of coal. Nowadays, the burning of coal is illegal in many cities.

In Victorian Britain, "King Coal" ruled a smoky kingdom. The clank and hiss of coal-fired steam engines echoed across factories, mines, and workshops, while at home, heating and cooking was done on coal fires and ranges.

Mining mayhem

Demand for coal soared during the 19th century. In 1800, around 12 million tons were mined, but by 1900 this was a vast 225 million tons. As coal near the surface was used up, mines became deeper and more dangerous.

Most years, over 1,000 miners died in accidents, usually from roof collapses. Sometimes they perished in dreadful disasters that wiped out dozens or even hundreds of men. The worst came in December 1866, at the Oaks Colliery near Barnsley. Two gas explosions killed 361 miners and a rescue party of 27.

Vexing vapors

Victorian cities were sheathed in smoke from millions of coal fires. Manchester was compared to an active volcano; Charles Dickens called the smoke "London ivy that wreathed itself around every building." So far so bad, but when smoke mixed with wet fog it became a killer — smog.

Often, it was impossible to see across the street and most winters the death rate soared.

Cor blimey, gov! — Pea-soupers

Victorians didn't use the word smog. They called the creepy mixture of smoke and fog a pea-souper. Why? Because the air was often a thick, greeny/browny/yellowish color — like pea soup.

In 1886, a dense smog choked London on February 9 and 10. It was so thick that the poor poured out of their slums to loot West End shops and over 12,000 people died from bronchitis.

Horrific Houses

Even the curtains were poisonous!

Victorian towns and cities became more and more squalid. As people poured in from the countryside to find work, populations soared. Glasgow rocketed from 77,000 people in 1801 to 522,000 in 1871 and Manchester from 75,000 to 351,000.

Super slums

Houses for these new workers were often jerry-built and crowded closely together, without drains or running water. They became instant slums, feared as *fever dens* where cholera lurked or *rookeries* that hid violent criminals.

The Nichol was a notorious slum in London. The houses were thrown up cheaply using cement that never set, and walls without foundations, made from half-baked bricks. These houses weren't just damp – they were soggy from the start.

Meanwhile in Manchester, a shocked inspector found 16 cottages in Deansgate:

...inhabited by 16 men, 21 women and 33 children making a total of 70 persons. The 5 cellars are inhabited by another 24 persons. Total 94 persons.

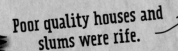

Poor quality houses and slums were rife.

14

Argh, no paper!

94 people using just 2 toilets – phwoar!

VERY VEXING VICTORIANS
Death on the walls

Green was all the rage in the mid-19th century and any house-proud Victorian had to have a green room. But the brilliant green color came from arsenic-based dyes... and so did blue, yellow and brown.

In the Limehouse area of London in 1861, three children in the same family died within weeks of one another from the symptoms of diphtheria: sore throats, fever, and tiredness. But further investigation showed they had been poisoned by arsenic vapor – from the wallpaper in their bedroom.

Cor blimey, gov!
One wallpaper manufacturer estimated that there were 155 million square miles (250 million sq km) of arsenic-colored wallpapers in British houses in 1858!

And they all shared just two toilets – start lining up now.

Posh problems

Better-off people moved away from the dirty town centers to the suburbs. However, their new homes were full of hidden killers. From the 1840s, every town had a gas works, piping coal gas into houses for lighting. This contained hydrogen, which is highly explosive, and carbon monoxide, which is toxic. What a double whammy!

If there was a leak, there was a risk of explosion, but more commonly people suffocated in badly ventilated rooms. And then there was lead poisoning from pipes and paint, children falling into open fires and arsenic in curtain fabrics. Let us OUT!

Sometimes it was safer to leave the lights off...

Can I smell G...

Rotten Railways

Definitely no running on the platform, please, with this patented...

Rubber bladder

Leg strap

The pee collects in here. Lovely.

When Victoria became Queen of England, there were over 1,400 miles (2,300 km) of railway line in Britain. Incredibly, by her death, there were over 1,800 miles (30,000 km). Traveling had never been so easy — but was everybody happy? You can bet your life they weren't.

Nifty navvies

The railways were built by thousands of navvies — tough laborers who constructed vast cuttings, embankments, tunnels, and viaducts with muscle, shovels and blasting powder. The navvies lived in shantytowns alongside the new lines and had a reputation for hard drinking and fighting. Diseases ripped through these crude

Cor blimey, gov!

It took 6,000 navvies five years to build the 68-mile-long (110-km-long) Settle-to-Carlisle line in the 1870s. The line has 14 tunnels and 16 viaducts.

Probably best not to keep fireworks in your suitcase, then...

camps, killing dozens, while others suffered horrific injuries at work — caught in explosions or crushed by landslides.

Flaming luggage

Until the 1860s, railway carriages looked like stagecoaches on tracks. They were divided into compartments, but there were no corridors — and no toilets or buffet cars. Passengers had to cross their legs until the train stopped at a larger station, or pee into rubber bladders hidden under their clothes. Luggage was stored on carriage roofs and sometimes caught fire from hot cinders blown back by the engine.

The runaway train

Victorian railways were surprisingly safe, but every now and then there were some spectacular disasters.

The most famous was the collapse of the Tay Bridge in 1879. A section of the bridge fell in hurricane–force winds, just as a train was crossing. At least 60 people were killed.

The worst accident came 10 years later, near Armagh in Northern Ireland. Runaway carriages, from a Sunday school outing, careered back down the line and smashed into an oncoming train. Eighty were killed and around 260 injured, including many children.

VERY VEXING VICTORIANS

The Tay Bridge disaster

Beautiful Railway Bridge of the Silv'ry Tay!
Alas! I am very sorry to say
That ninety lives have been taken away
On the last Sabbath day of 1879,
Which will be remember'd for a very long time.

By William McGonagall. William has been called the world's worst poet. What do you think?

Cor blimey, gov! Historical humor

I say boy, what is the quickest way to the railway-station?

Run, Sir.

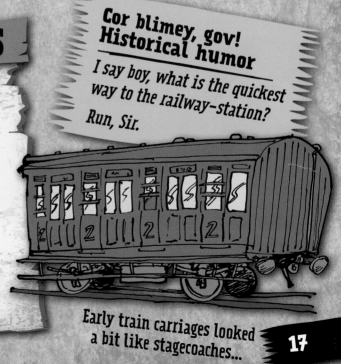

Early train carriages looked a bit like stagecoaches...

Horrible Hospitals and Dirty Doctors

Florence Nightingale taught nurses to keep notes on patients.

Er, hello?

Imagine a time when going into the hospital was almost a death sentence and patients had to be strapped down before an operation — to stop them running away. Welcome to early Victorian medical care.

Wicked wards

In the early 19th century, most hospitals were called infirmaries and run by charities. Nurses were untrained and wards filthy and overcrowded. Bedding was rarely changed and patients shared bucket toilets with staff. No wonder diseases spread easily and infected wounds became killer conditions.

Florence Nightingale helped transform these wards.

In 1860, she set up the first training school for nurses at St. Thomas' Hospital, London. Nurses were taught to observe the sick carefully, keep records and above all, to keep the wards clean. *The first requirement in a hospital*, Florence wrote, *is that it should do the sick no harm.*

Speedy surgeons

In the 1830s, having an operation was a seriously painful problem. There were no anesthetics to kill pain or antiseptics to prevent infections. Top surgeons such as Robert Liston worked fast to prevent blood loss and could amputate a leg in just 30 seconds. With blood jetting in all directions, most surgeons wore their oldest coats to work. After all,

what was the point of spoiling a good clean jacket?

The first British operation using ether as an anesthetic took place in 1846. But it wasn't until 1865 that Joseph Lister used carbolic acid as an antiseptic.

Early Victorian wards were a bit overcrowded...

Doctor Robert Liston didn't waste time. He could hack off – sorry, amputate – a leg in just 30 seconds.

Ready sir? 3, 2, 1...

VERY VEXING VICTORIANS

Awesome antiseptics

On August 12, 1865, a boy named James Greenlees, aged 11, was admitted with compound fracture of the left leg caused by the wheel of a cart. The treatment consisted of careful application of undiluted carbolic acid to all parts of the wound which was then dressed with lint, soaked in the same fluid. Under the dressing, the blood and carbolic acid formed a protective crust beneath which the wound began to heal.

Report by Dr. Lister, 1865

Thomas Crapper and Troubled Toilets

Early flush toilets suffered from odor problems.

Early Victorian streets were messy and stinky! Human and animal waste was dumped in the streets or emptied into stinking cess pits and middens — ponds or piles of poop. Something had to be done.

Toilet wars

Some cities, such as London, built grand sewage systems and connected a network of water closets, or WCs, to them. But there were problems with early toilet designs. The stink from the sewers seeped back through the pipes and left householders holding their noses.

Victorian streets were a right old mess, with poops, bum plops, turds and tinkles everywhere.

Enter a rival toilet invented by Dorset vicar Henry Moule: the earth closet. Instead of water, soil (earth), or ashes were put on the poo — and instead of flushing into sewers, the ECs were emptied by gangs of nightsoil men. Even better, the poop mix could be sold to farmers as fertilizer.

Earth closets were cheaper to install than building sewerage systems and as late as 1900, major cities such as Manchester had more ECs than WCs. But don't laugh — the posh name for earth closets is composting toilets, and they are still in use all over the world.

Flushed!

In London, however, things were a little different. The Great Stink of 1858 brought the city to its knees for a few hot summer days — the stench from the River Thames and the smelly streets became unbearable.

Parliament decided that more sewers had to be built and all new houses were to be fitted with WCs. An advance in design now also meant that WCs no longer allowed the stench to seep back through the pipes. Eventually, other cities followed London's lead.

Emptying ashpits in Bolton

One man went ahead opening the ashpit doors, and dragging out the ash tubs, all ready for his two mates coming up behind, who would drag the pail out, empty it into the cart and then replace it. Following on behind them was a man who swept up and shut the ashpit doors and generally made the back street tidy.

Remembered by Bill Naughton, novelist.

Now don't say I never give you anything, farmer Giles.

Thank ye kindly, sir!

What do you give the farmer who has everything? A steaming bucket of plop, of course!

Foul Food

It took as many as 30 sparrows to make a pie!

Victorian children weren't picky eaters — their big problem was getting enough food in the first place. Compared to people today, Victorians were small, sickly, undernourished, and really rickety. Hard-working adults burned up around 3,500 calories a day and obese people were so unusual they could make a living as fairground freaks.

My my, eel and sparrow pie

Eating well was impossible for many. Poor families not only struggled to buy food, they had no cooking facilities. The sole source of heat was an open fire and many had just one pan that sometimes doubled as a chamber pot at night!

In cities, people often lived off street food — mutton or eel pies, hot pea soup, and muffins. From the 1880s, fish and chips became a favorite, cheap and nutritious meal.

Did you wash the pan?

I thought you did...

Some families were so poor they peed and cooked in the same pan!

Surprisingly, many farm workers went hungry, too. Their basic foods were bread, butter, beer, and potatoes, with meat a rare treat. Rabbits and wild birds, such as sparrows, were trapped for pies and stews. It took as many as 30 sparrows to make a family stew and every bird had to be plucked and skinned.

Seedy sweets

Even the richest Victorians faced the peril of adulterated foods. Until the 1870s, there were no effective food laws and many food manufacturers tried to save money by adding cheap but sketchy ingredients.

Poisons were common. Strychnine gave beer a bitter taste, red lead turned Gloucester cheese a "healthy" red and mercury bisulphate was used to make brightly colored sweets. Yummy! Sweets that could rot your teeth and tummy at the same time!

VERY VEXING VICTORIANS
Foul food additives
Cross these off your grocery list!

Food	Awful additives
milk	chalk
white bread	alum, chalk
coffee	chicory, dried and ground peas and beans, burnt sugar
tea leaves	dust, used tea leaves
sausages	diseased meat
meat pies	sawdust
beer	water, treacle, salt strychnine
sweets	bright colors from lead, copper, and mercury

Cor blimey, gov!

Around 200 people died in Bradford in 1858 when a local sweet seller, Humbug Billy, added arsenic to his humbug mix. Billy Hardaker had meant to add plaster of Paris to save money on sugar, but the chemist gave him the wrong white powder. Ooops.

Killer Corsets and Mad Makeup

Fancy a 16" waist, ladies? To be honest, we're not sure it's worth it...

Victorian women faced some formidable fashions. In the 1850s the killer look was a narrow waist, but wide skirts from the hip down. So, to seem alluring, fashion dictated being dome shaped. Call in the corsets and crinolines!

Killer corsets

Corsets were cotton or silk underwear, reinforced with whale bones to shape the body. They were large, stiff, and constricting. Girls had to be trained to wear corsets from childhood — sometimes as young as five.

Corsets were laced at the back and gave an elegant, slim look to the wearer. The problems started if they were fastened too tightly. Then it became difficult for a woman to breathe, bend or even sit down comfortably. At worst, internal organs such as the liver and lungs were damaged.

Petticoat peril

As well as coping with corsets, women faced petticoat perils. In the 1840s, skirts were pushed out by as many as six starched and stiffened petticoats. These became so heavy that even walking was a challenge.

In the 1850s, the Americans invented the crinoline — a lightweight metal cage that hung from a band round the waist. Now skirts hung over this contraption could be even wider, but at least they were lighter. Men joked that it was impossible for two ladies to walk together through a door without a crash.

Cor blimey, gov!

Many of the appalling additives in food ended up in cosmetics, too. Face washes that promised to remove blemishes certainly did – with poisonous arsenic (again!), bichloride of mercury, and hydrochloric acid. But hey, they came scented with rose water to hide the chemical smell. Some face creams, designed to hide wrinkles, contained white lead – a slow poison that can be absorbed through the skin. Perfect.

VERY VEXING
VICTORIANS

Tight-laced torture

By the 1890s, the fad for an ultra thin "wasp waist" was at its height. The terrifying target for a young fashionista was to measure just 16 inches round the middle. Doctors despaired at the results.

Slightly serious symptoms:
breathlessness; fainting; aching back; high blood pressure

Severely serious symptoms:
weak back and stomach muscles; crushed or broken ribs; miscarriages (yes, some women did tighten their corsets while they were pregnant); blood supply to the liver cut off

Hello there. Ever heard of the jolly Christian faith? We have seats and everything!

Cruel Britannia: Wicked Wars

By 1900, the British Empire was the largest in history. And, according to the Victorians, brought great benefits to those lucky enough to be conquered: the English language, trade, Christian faith, government, and railways. Those peoples forced into the Empire had a different story to tell — that of Cruel Britannia.

Mighty Indian mutiny

By the 1850s, the British had managed to colonize most of the Indian subcontinent; but they were in for a shock. In 1857, regiments of native troops in the Indian army mutinied and shot their British officers. When the Brits took control again, they wanted revenge — wiping out villages and executing thousands of mutineers. The Indians called this the *Devil's Wind*.

Some former British colonies still have the Union Jack as part of their flag.

British cruelty was remembered and inspired the Indian independence movement in the 20th century.

Zulus and Boers

From the 1870s, the British were determined to control South Africa, which meant fighting native Zulu warriors and the Boers (descendants of Dutch-speaking settlers). In 1879, they initially attacked Zululand, expecting a walkover.

Instead, at the Battle of Isandlwana, a force of 20,000 warriors, armed with spears, wiped out a British army equipped with modern rifles. The British won the war eventually, with the help of artillery and the latest Gatling guns.

By 1899, the Brits were taking on the Boers — and losing. Around 250,000 British Empire troops were killed in a war with 30,000 Boers. In the end, the British won with terrible tactics.

Boer farms were burned and families rounded up and held in concentration camps. The camps were badly run, and 26,000 Boer women and children died from diseases caused by poor sanitation.

Bloemfontein Concentration Camp

I saw crowds in bitterly cold weather, in pouring rain – hungry, sick, dying and dead. The water supply was inadequate. No bedstead or mattress was procurable. Fuel was scarce and had to be collected from the green bushes on the slopes of the kopjes (small hills). The rations were extremely meager and simply meant famine.

Emily Hobhouse, 1901.

Emily Hobhouse was a British campaigner who fought to have Boer concentration camps closed.

Zulu warriors were pretty nifty at aiming with spears

But Sarge...

Don't shoot until you can see the whites of their eyes!

Fine Funerals

Victorians used elaborate symbols on their grave stones. Take a look at our grave guide to find out what the cross and anchor symbolize.

There was a lot of death around in the 19th century. And as they couldn't dodge it, the Victorians decided to indulge in it. The dearly departed were sent on their way with the finest funerals.

Curtains and clocks

In most families, the dead were usually kept at home until the funeral. This was to allow relatives and friends to pay their last respects — and just in case the person was only in a coma.

One of the more humble funeral processions...

Curtains were drawn and clocks stopped, while mirrors were covered with black crêpe — just in case the deceased's spirit was in danger of becoming trapped in the glass.

Wealthy families had elaborate funerals. The hearse was black, pulled by black horses and decorated with a huge canopy of black ostrich feathers. The mourners rode in coaches with the blinds pulled down — the more coaches the better.

Cor blimey, gov!

Poorer families paid weekly into burial clubs even if this left them short of food. They were desperate to avoid the disgrace of a cheap pauper funeral with an unmarked grave.

This grand procession moved at walking pace through the main streets to the cemetery. After the service there was a feast — hot soup, ham, pies, and cakes.

Royal remembrance

When Queen Victoria's beloved husband, Albert, died in 1861, the Royal Household went against the fashion of the time and conducted a very intimate, low-key funeral for the deceased Prince Consort.

The Queen was heartbroken and wore black — the color of mourning — for the rest of her life. Albert's rooms were left exactly as he liked them and servants fetched hot water for his shave every morning. Victoria was nicknamed the *Widow of Windsor* and was buried wearing her wedding veil.

Angel – a guide to heaven

Grave Guide

You don't have to be a vampire to enjoy a walk through a Victorian cemetery. Look out for these symbols on the grave stones:

Anchor – hope of eternal life

Angel – a guide to heaven

Birds flying – souls going to heaven

Broken column – a life, often the head of the family (Dad)

Cross – salvation in Christ

Eye – all-seeing God

Lamb – innocence or Christ the redeemer (often found on a child's grave)

Scythe or sickle – time

Skull – death

Trumpeters – sounding the resurrection

Glossary

calcium chloride: an early disinfectant

Cor blimey, gov: Victorian expression of surprise, from the much older phrase "God blind me"

compound fracture: a bone broken so badly that it pokes though the skin, allowing infection

concentration camps: places to lock up huge amounts of enemy civilians at the same time. They were not designed as death camps, but many inmates died because they were badly run.

empire: the lands ruled by Britain

ether: a gas that can be used to anesthetize

flue: a channel inside a chimney. Victorian chimneys usually had several flues.

Gatling guns: early machine guns

hearse: the carriage that carried the coffin

Indian subcontinent: modern India, Bangladesh and Pakistan

jerry-built: badly constructed

loom: a machine that weaves thread or yarn into fabric

music hall: like a theater that showed variety acts – everything from circus performers to singers

navvies: short for navigators. The name was given to the men who built the canals, but stuck as a name for the railway builders.

opium: a powerful drug made from poppies. Victorian doctors prescribed opium for all sorts of ailments.

patent: to officially register an invention as your own

pauper funeral: the cheapest funeral paid by the Poor Law Guardians

pits: mines

range: a coal- or coke-fueled cooker

rickety: affected by rickets, which is a disease caused by vitamin D deficiency. Bones become soft and deformed, resulting in bowed legs.

rookeries: city slums. The name was taken from the noisy, packed nesting areas of rooks.

skivvy: a maid who did all jobs around the house

soot: black dust from fires

viaducts: railway bridges

weaning: gradually moving babies from milk to solid food

workhouse: a large building where poor people who asked for support had to live

More information

Places to visit

Henry B. Plant Museum, Tampa, Florida
Originally built as the Tampa Bay Hotel in 1891 by railroad magnate Henry Bradley Plant, today the Plant Museum is a wonderful example of Gilded Age architecture and houses an assortment of Victorian era furnishings. And you can take part in a Victorian Christmas Stroll during the holidays.
http://plantmuseum.com

Black Country Living Museum, Dudley, UK
This open air museum allows to you wander Victorian streets and chat to its residents!
www.bclm.co.uk/index.htm

The Florence Nightingale Museum, London, UK
An exhibition that spans Nightingale's life and even includes her pet owl Athena!
www.florence-nightingale.co.uk

Websites

http://www.pbs.org/wnet/1900house/index.html
PBS's The 1900 House brings a modern-day family back in time to live in a Victorian house the way people lived in 1900.

www.bbc.co.uk/schools/primaryhistory/victorian_britain
A fun website about all things Victorian, with some interesting activities.

www.bl.uk/learning/histcitizen/victorians/victorianhome.html
A great site from the British Library. Try the fascinating slideshows and podcasts.

cookit.e2bn.org/
Browse through the Victorian pages of the History Cookbook. We dare you to try the recipe for gruel: cookit.e2bn.org/historycookbook/121-gruel.html

Publisher's note to educators and parents: Our editors have carefully reviewed these websites to ensure that they are suitable for students. Many websites change frequently, however, and we cannot guarantee that a site's future contents will continue to meet our high standards of quality and educational value. Be advised that students should be closely supervised whenever they access the Internet.

Books

Oliver Twist by Charles Dickens; ebook available free online from the Gutenberg Project

Victorian Workers Turned Dog Poo into Gold! – The Fact or Fiction Behind the Victorians by Peter Hepplewhite, Wayland (2014)

The Gruesome Truth About The Victorians by Jillian Powell, Wayland (2012)

Index